Married

Marriage Devotions
with Realistic Challenges
from the Christian Perspective

By: Michael Marler

ISBN # 9798740806259

Scripture References: KJV/NKJV

To my Beautiful wife Brandy.
Thanks for all the inspiration.

Before you Begin

I hope you picked up this book with high expectations for the future of your marriage. I expect that you want your marriage to succeed. I desire mine to. The fantastic news for both of us is that God wants to see our marriages succeed. I believe marriage is from the mind of God and that He has a deep love and passion for it. At an early age, I discovered that I loved the idea of marriage. The concept seemed simple, yet highly rewarding. As I got into my upper teen years, I began to look forward to a day I would have a wife of my own. I got married to my beautiful wife Brandy when I was twenty and I have never lost my love and passion for it. My marriage like everyone else's has seen its fair share of struggles, and that's ok. Marriage was not designed to make life perfect but designed to help imperfect people successfully navigate through life. That is what my marriage has done for me. That is what I want your marriage to do for you. Marriage testifies of a greater life and teaches us a great deal about God. In Ephesians chapter five, Paul teaches that the relationship of marriage between a man and woman reflects the relationship of Christ and His church. Through His example, we can have the same kind of passion, love, and intimacy that He has with his people. The relationship we have with God is a constant journey that requires sacrifice and commitment. God gave us His word to help us with life's struggles and to find the ability to relate to Him, even in our darkest moments. As we use God's word and its principles to relate to him, we can also use them to relate to one another. Marriage is a journey that requires the same kind of sacrifice and commitment. I believe that is one of the points Paul was making in Ephesians chapter five. Practice using God's word and its principles in your own homes;

with the ones that are closest to you. Let them teach you how to have a successful relationship, a successful life, and a successful walk with God. I hope that as you read this book and practice its advice that you would find purpose and identity in your marriage. Try not to shy away from the challenges. Marriage should challenge you. It should produce a better you. If it is not, then you are doing it wrong. I hope that you come to realize that every day is an opportunity to learn from your spouse and an opportunity to love them as Christ does. Allow your marriage the opportunity to teach you.

Each devotion will be more effective if you and your spouse read and pray through it together. If you can't, that's ok. You can read and pray through it by yourself. Read the devotions as often as you see fit but try to complete the challenge associated with your current devotion before you move on to the next one. Keep an open mind and have fun.

List of Devotions

1. He Needed Her
2. The Umbrella Effect
3. Better
4. The Power Of Investment
5. The Key To Happiness
6. Everybody Poops
7. What's Love Got To Do With It?
8. Submit
9. Agreed
10. Marriage Is A Garden, Dig It
11. Say What?
12. Learn To Lose
13. That's Random
14. Absence Makes The Heart Grow Peaceful
15. Thank You
16. Freedom In The Bedroom
17. Microscopic
18. That Time Of The Month
19. Live, Laugh, Stay Married
20. Your Feet Smell Good
21. Tipping The Scales
22. Take Pride In Me
23. Write The Vision
24. Limits
25. Tag, Your It
26. Remember

27. Good Hurt
28. Offense Vs. Defense
29. Hold My Hand
30. Empowered Leadership
31. Pillow Talk
32. Irreconcilable Differences
33. Slippery Slope
34. Holy Perfection
35. Spill Your Guts
36. Heaven
37. Beautiful
38. The Old File Cabinet
39. Stuck Like Glue
40. Will You Trust Me?
41. I Need A Vacation
42. Taco Tuesday
43. Revelation
44. Wise Counsel

1. He Needed Her

To start grasping the purpose of something, we must look at its beginning. Marriage has been around a long time and there is much to learn from its history. Let's start with its birth. Let's look back at Adam and Eve. Is it by chance that the covenant of marriage was established before the fall of mankind? Or was this by supreme design? The argument could be said that Adam fell because Eve disobeyed God's commandment and caused him to fall. Men love to throw that in women's faces. But the question is; would he have fallen all by himself, eventually? Have you ever pondered that question? In James 1:14 it says, "But every man is tempted, when he is drawn away of his own lust, and enticed." So, in the realm of our susceptibility to lust and sin, we are all on the same playing field. Adam was no different than Eve when it came to his ability to be tempted.

This leads me to believe that Adam would have disobeyed God eventually on his own. God did not create Eve to make Adam fall. He knew that Adam would fall, and that he would need her when he did.

We are tempted to blame others; especially those closest to us, for our mistakes and failures. That was Adam's go to. He quickly blamed Eve for his mistake when God confronted him. This is a very immature way of facing our problems. We need to stop blaming our spouse for our difficulties and take ownership of them. Our true need in marriage is not to find someone to share the blame, but someone who will help us recover what we have lost. You will go through hard times with or without your marriage. Why not let your marriage do what God designed it to do and help you through those struggles. When Adam and Eve sinned they lost everything, and they lost it together. The family is built upon a foundation of commitment that says, no matter what, we can get through this together. Didn't you desire that kind of family when you said I do? The sad reality is that many marriages today quickly fall apart over the ordinary struggles of life. God created the institution of marriage before the sin and fall of mankind. When all the sin, mistakes, and disappointments happened, the covenant of marriage did not fall apart. It fell together.

The Challenge

Think about your mistakes and struggles in life that you tend to take out on your spouse. Is there anything that you need to take ownership of that you have not? Take pen and paper and make a list of the circumstances in life where you would be thankful your spouse was with you. Take your time and fill up the paper. Pray that God would give your marriage the strength and maturity to fall together and not apart.

2. The Umbrella Effect

How close to a married life did you live with your spouse before you were actually married? Did you live together? Did you share your finances? Did you have sex? Did you have children? I know, I know, this is the modern world. I have had couples actually tell me that they needed to test drive the car before they made the purchase. I understand the point they are making but there is a problem with their rationale and I call it the umbrella effect. In Genesis 2:24 Moses records, "Therefore shall a man leave his father and his mother, and shall cleave unto his wife: and they shall be one flesh." Biblically the act of becoming one is in sync with the act of marriage. The man and the women leave their separate lives to begin a new life together. This is all done under the umbrella of God's covenant of marriage. Now what does an umbrella do? If it's a good umbrella, it should protect you from the storm. Everything under the umbrella stays dry while everything outside of it is subject to the weather. When a couple lives like they are married before they are, they fail to protect the lives they have built with the promises of God's covenant. They are also building a life without God's support. God honors marriage. I think most people wait so long to get married because they don't see the point in it. They may say, "We already live like we are married so why should we get married." And if they eventually get married, little to nothing changes in their lives. This is a major problem. If nothing changes when you get married; what does marriage actually mean to you? You are treating it as if it means little to nothing to you. I'm not saying you didn't care what God thought about your relationship or that you don't care about your marriage. I simply want you to think about how much you rely on God and how accountable you hold yourself to His covenant of marriage. We can't go back and change anything. If you lived partly or fully like you were married before you were then what's done is done. You just have to recognize those things not protected and work hard to get them under the umbrella. Don't let a simple rainstorm wash away what you have worked so hard to build. Marriage starts with a promise. Everything you go through as a couple should always find its foundation upon that promise. One thing is for sure, the storm is coming. Get all parts of your relationship under the umbrella and let God help you protect them from the storm when it strikes.

The Challenge

Go grab an umbrella and sit under it. I know it's silly. Just do it. As you both sit under the umbrella discuss everything you have built together and how you lived before you were married. Evaluate what you have learned and if steps need to be taken to get certain things under the umbrella. Pray that God will protect every part of your relationship from the storms of life and that your umbrella stays strong.

3. "Better"

How do you define success in your marriage? When you look at other couples, how do you gauge the greatness of their marriage? In the book of Ecclesiastes 7:8 the bible reads, "Better is the end of a thing than the beginning thereof: and the patient in spirit is better than the proud in spirit." To put this in simple terms regarding marriage we could say; things are better when they last. I am not saying that simply the length of time makes a great marriage. If a marriage has lasted sixty years but the couple was mean and hateful to each other the whole time, then I would say it was a failure. True greatness in marriage is when the end is just as good if not better than the beginning. I think that it is safe to say that most marriages start well. I wouldn't have gotten married if my relationship was not in a good place. But the reality of marriages today is that many of them don't finish well. Many end in divorce or linger in misery. When you think about it, it is much better to finish well than begin well. So, how do we get to this place called "Better"? The second half of the verse tells us how to get there. Better is the patient in spirit than the proud in spirit. Any marriage that will stand the test of time and come out better will require tons and tons of patience. To succeed at anything in life it takes patience. I would love to learn how to play the piano. With enough time, energy, and patience I could get good at it. But the problem is, I have never taken the time to learn. I have never felt it was worth it. Is that a problem in your marriage? Is it worth your time, energy and patience? If you believe it is, then your marriage has great potential for "better". Pride is always at odds with your marriage. To be proud in spirit is to have an attitude and view that everything is about you and how you feel. Marriage is God's gift to us to help kill this kind of pride within our spirit. Biblical marriage is about making your spouse's life better, and in return your life will become better. My hopes for my marriage and for yours are that every year that passes we can say, this year is better than the last.

The Challenge

Think about the time period of your marriage. When was it at its greatest? Why was it great then? Come up with some short- and long-term goals that will make your spouse's life better. Pray that God will teach you to exercise a patient spirit towards your spouse and that God will help your marriage become better with time.

4. The Power Of Investment

We all have material things that we invest in. My house and cars are investments. I have invested time and money into them because of the benefit of having them. I try to take care of these things because it was my money, earned with my hard work that paid for them. The fact that I am personally invested empowers me to not only care about these things but to care for them. God uses tithing to teach us the power of an investment. He asks us to give a tenth of our income to the ministry so that it can prosper and help those it is called upon to help. But tithing is also for you. God loves a cheerful giver. Giving brings joy and a sense of purpose to our lives. But God knows and hopefully you do too, that the more you invest into the ministry, the more you will care for it. The people that tithe in the church are also usually the people that serve. They have a vested interest in the success of the ministry. In the Gospel of Matthew 6:21 it says "For where your treasure is, there will your heart be also." Your heart follows your money or the things you treasure. Now let's think about our marriages considering this principle. The more I invest of my treasure into my marriage, the more I will care about it. Let me ask you this question. If God spoke to you and told you to give your car away for free to someone who needed it; would it be easier to give away a car you paid five hundred dollars for or a car you paid fifty thousand dollars for? It would be much harder to walk away from a fifty-thousand-dollar car. Is it easier to walk away from a church you have invested zero dollars as opposed to a church you gave ten thousand dollars to last year? Marriage works by the same principle. The more I invest, the harder it is to walk away. You should be so invested in your marriage that the slightest hint of failure should drive you to action. When the hint of failure comes, we should stand our ground and say; we have come too far, we have spent too much time and money to let this go. Your heart and your treasure move together. Let them both move in the best interest of your marriage. If I am really going to love my spouse and my children like God has called me to, then I must be willing to invest.

The Challenge

How hard would it be for you right now to walk away from your marriage? The answer to that may give you some insight on exactly how invested in it you are. List the ways you have personally invested in your marriage and come up with a few more ways you can invest. Pray that God will teach you how to give cheerfully not only to Him but also to your spouse.

5. The Key To Happiness

What have you found to be the key to happiness in your life? I'm not just talking about things that make you happy. Many things give us momentary pleasures. I am speaking more to a happiness that is attached to your lifestyle and character. The key to happiness is contentment. Anyone can learn how to live in a state of contentment. I think we can safely say that money itself can't bring lasting happiness. If that were true, then rich people would be the happiest people in the world. They have the same problems everyone else has, and some worse. Ecclesiastes 6:9 states "Better is the sight of the eyes than the wandering of the desire…" The truth is that we are usually convinced that there is something better out there. We convince ourselves the grass is greener somewhere else or with someone else. I don't care if you are rich, poor or middle class; we all chase our desires. This is the nature of our flesh. But here we have a challenge by the writer to take note of what is right in front of you. Take a look at your marriage. Look at what is in arm's length of you. This is what you have the power to be happy in. We are fooled into thinking that our happiness is going to be found at the end of our desires, but we will never reach that end. When things in life get hard, we are tempted to imagine ourselves living differently. We tell ourselves there is a relationship out there that wouldn't be so difficult and more rewarding.
People that act on these imaginations usually find themselves in the same position in life, just with another person. I do not believe that marriage is all about happiness. This is a Hollywood type mentality. It says, if this person doesn't make you happy then go get another person. News flash, you will not always be happy in marriage. Happiness comes as a benefit of doing marriage

right. We will all fall short and make mistakes. Contentment is something we learn together. My wife and I are different people than we were when we got married. We have developed into what we are today. There have been numerous growing pains in that development. We have both grown in contentment and learned to appreciate who is standing in front of us. This is a state of happiness any marriage can find if they are willing to turn the key.

The Challenge

Have a discussion with your spouse about what makes you both happy. Challenge each other to recognize the blessings in your life and the things you should be thankful for. Pray that God will teach you contentment when your marriage is good and when it's not. Pray that He will reveal the things right in front of you that you are failing to see.

6. Everybody Poops

When my children were learning how to use the potty my wife Brandy got a book called "Everybody Poops". The book shows many different types of animals (for lack of better words) pooping. The point is to show how normal it is. It's not a big deal to have to use the bathroom because everyone does it. Now what does this have to do with marriage? In the book of Proverbs Solomon declares "Where no oxen are, the crib is clean: but much increase is by the strength of the ox."(14:4) Do you ever think that life would be easier without your spouse? You wouldn't have to pick up after them or make plans that accommodate them. Sometimes it is a lot of work and uses up a lot of your energy sharing this life with someone. Just like the Proverb, there are benefits to not having the ox or the spouse. However, there is much increase by the strength of the ox, or the spouse. We can get caught up in the negatives of having our spouse around and fail to appreciate how they add to our lives. Have you ever had a pet that you had to clean up after? If you kept that animal, you must have believed that the animal was worth it. You enjoyed having it enough to deal with the fact that you had to clean up after it. Marriage works the same way. Is your spouse worth it to you? There was a time you believed they were. Our relationships usually start out with a lot of positive thinking. We overlook the things we don't like about the other person because we have decided to love them. As our marriages move forward, we can tend to overlook the positives and focus on the negatives. This can become a toxic frame of mind within your marriage. I believe as our marriages began, we challenged ourselves to love our spouses. We purposefully loved them for who they were. I believe many people think their problems are unique to them. People say, "no one else goes through this". If you have said that before, I am happy to say, you're wrong. Everyone struggles on some level. Everyone poops, and you know what; it's normal. So, love them even when it is difficult, and love will do exactly what God designed it to do.

The Challenge

Think about the beginning of your relationship. Think about the reasons you believed your spouse was worth your love and devotion. Vocalize those reasons (go ahead and do it). A mature marriage doesn't overlook the negatives in your spouse and pretend they aren't there. A mature marriage learns how to love despite those negatives. Challenge yourself to see the worth of your marriage and pray that God would teach you how to love even when it's difficult.

7. What's Love Got To Do With It?

Is there such a thing as falling in love? Hollywood certainly thinks so. Many movies portray a couple that falls madly in love with each other despite all the forces that try to keep them apart. We can get too caught up in this way of thinking about love. Is it really some magical force that we simply fall into? The problem with looking at love this way is that when things start going wrong in the relationship, you can start to believe it's just not meant to be. We can start doubting the forces that brought us together. Love is not a magic trick. It is not something we fall into. It is certainly not something we fall out of. Love is a choice. It will always be a choice. If you were to say, "I don't love my spouse anymore", it would be because you have chosen not to. There is no magical force that has caused you to feel this way. Is there ever a time in life that God is ok with you no longer loving your spouse? Is there something they can do or say that gives you this right? Let's look at some scripture for some clarification in this area. Matthew 5:43 and 44 says, "You have heard that it was said, 'you shall love your neighbor and hate your enemy.' But I say unto you, love your enemies, bless those who curse you, do good to those that hate you, and pray for those who spitefully use you and persecute you." If it is God's will that you love your enemies, what do you think He believes about the way you should love your spouse?

This is not an easy bible passage to swallow for most people. We like to believe that we can justify our feelings of hate or dislike for someone. This scripture was meant to shake you up. It grabs you by the shoulders and shouts, LOVE IS A CHOICE. It is easy to hate an enemy. It takes great self-control, patience, and humility to love them, pray for them, and do good to them. Love shines at its greatest when it is put to the test. When it hangs on in the darkest of storms. Even when it hangs on a cross. I know that the storms of a marriage can get pretty ugly. Certain circumstances warrant you getting away from your spouse. Abuse of any kind should not be tolerated. But love is still a choice; no matter the circumstances. It is not possible to fall out of love. People simply develop a change of heart over time. They stop performing acts of love. They neglect one another and start to wonder what went wrong. Love is an action word. Love is not found in an accidental fall. It is found in an intentional walk. Walk it out with your spouse. See how far it can take you. I guarantee you have not reached its potential.

The Challenge

Watch an appropriate movie you both like that has some type of love story in it. Action movies have love stories as well ladies. Discuss the differences in the way the world teaches us to love and how God teaches us to love. Pray for your spouse and ask God to teach you how to love your spouse as He does.

8. Submit

Submit; does anybody like that word? I have been in those church services when the scripture is read that a wife should submit to her husband. You can just feel the room get uncomfortable. Women start to cringe and whisper one to another. Most men and women think it is an unfair word. They may say, why should I submit to my spouse when they don't treat me right? Have you ever said or thought that? That scripture is in Ephesians 5:22 that reads "Wives, submit yourselves unto your own husbands, as unto the Lord." But let's look and focus on the verse right before it. In Ephesians 5:21 it reads, "Submitting yourselves to one another in the fear of God." Submitting, is something we are all called to do. In fact, the husband is told later in Ephesians to love his wife as Christ loved the church. Is this not a form of submission? Christ came not to be served but to serve his church. He sacrificed His own life so that his church could not only live but prosper. The husband is called to serve his wife and the wife is called to serve her husband. Success in marriage does not happen by being reactive to each other. If all our words and actions are reactive, we tend to let our emotions and feelings control them. Success comes when we are proactive in submitting to and loving our spouse. If we accept the attitude that we will not do our part until our mate does theirs, then we have created an atmosphere that will choke a marriage. For lack of time in this devotion we will not dissect everything this scripture is telling us, but I think we can expound on one point the writer is making. Maybe he is telling us what we need to hear. Perhaps the greatest struggle for a wife is to submit herself to her husband's authority and leadership. Perhaps the greatest struggle for a husband is to love his wife as Christ does and put her needs before his own. If we are honest, we can admit that this could be the case. Again, we are all called to submit and to love one another. Let's work on the areas we have the hardest time with. Submit is not a word given to us to hold us back or belittle us. It's a word when embraced, yields the best of results for our marriages. This is against our nature. Many times, submission even feels wrong. Push yourself to see past your selfish desires and take the scripture at its word.

The Challenge

The act of submitting to your spouse takes a lot of willpower to accomplish. Have a discussion about the positive outcome submission could have in your marriage. Talk about what submission looks like to you. You will be tempted to get negative but fight the urge and stay positive. Pray that God will teach you His idea of submission and how He wants your marriage to use it.

9. Agreed

Money has a way of stressing out a marriage like nothing else. Especially when the husband and wife don't look at money the same way. Usually in marriages there is a saver and a spender. The saver wants to see a lot of money stay in the bank account. The spender sees money in the account and thinks of a way to spend it. This simple difference in mindsets can cause marriages to stumble. Like with everything else in our marriages, we need to stand in agreement when it comes to money. Amos 3:3 says, "Can two walk together, except they be agreed?" This is a question the Lord asks His people. Can we walk together if we don't stand in agreement? The Lord wants to walk with you. Jesus died on the cross so that you could be saved and enter into a relationship with Him. When we begin a relationship with the Lord, we do so by making an agreement. A covenant relationship with Jesus is a binding agreement. We agree that we will put our faith in Him as Lord and Savior, and He agrees to give us new and abundant life. Didn't your marriage start with a binding agreement? Didn't you sign a contract called a marriage license? You promised to love and care for one another until separated by death. You would not have walked down the aisle together unless you made that agreement. The question God is asking is not up for interpretation. It is asked with an automatic answer. The answer is no. There are all kinds of challenges in marriage that causes us to not walk together. Money is perhaps the most challenging of all. Challenges like this can cause a marriage to lose its intimacy and make communication frustrating. So, stand in agreement. Just be careful not to stand in agreement to make horrible money choices. Debt upon debt will strangle you financially and relationally. Be smart. Make sure you

25

are both comfortable with the choices you are making with your money. This is regardless of who makes the money or the majority of it. You chose to be married. So, when it comes to your money; be married. Don't make quick financial decisions without consulting your spouse. Use time to your advantage. Many financial decisions would be different if people would slow down, pray and consider the aftermath of their spending. Don't try to keep up with the Jones'. They will always have better stuff than you.

The Challenge

Discuss which one of you is the saver and which one is the spender. How have you stood in agreement thus far in your marriage with money? Make a 5-year, 10-year or even 20-year plan on where you both want to be financially down the road. Pray and ask God to bless your money and help you make smart decisions with it that will benefit your marriage.

10. Marriage Is A Garden, Dig It

Have you ever grown a garden? If you have, you understand the struggle of dealing with the grass and weeds that always try to fill your garden. Usually I go on vacation for a week while the garden is in full swing. I come home to a weed infested garden that takes a lot of time and energy to fix. A successful garden requires regular tending and maintenance. A successful marriage requires the same thing. Solomon Talks about a vineyard in Proverbs 24:30-31. He says "I went by the field of the lazy man, and by the vineyard of the man devoid of understanding; and there it was, all overgrown with thorns; its surface was covered with needles; its stone wall was broken down." In his description, the condition of the man's vineyard was a direct result of his laziness and lack of understanding. But the point must be made that it was a vineyard. At one time it was a successful vineyard. What happened? Did the man no longer care about it? Did his passion for the vineyard simply fade away? I believe all of these reasons could be true. These reasons could also be used to describe a marriage that is failing. We did not begin our marriages to see them fall. At one time they were successful and rewarding. There was a vision in our heads of what it could one day be. So, what happened? What changed? Is yours still thriving, or did it get to difficult to keep up? To get the best out of my garden I have to work it regularly until the end. To get the best out of my marriage I must do the same. Sometimes our understanding fades. We don't see the importance and benefits of the marriage any longer. We get to a place where we no longer think it's worth it. Sometimes we simply get lazy. We think to ourselves; it is fine, there is nothing to worry about. But the thorns slowly creep in and the walls start to crumble. Before long, we look at our marriage as a chore and a burden. It becomes a place that is no longer beautiful; a place that we no longer want to share with each other. Be proactive to make your marriage a beautiful place that you both want to walk in. Like the garden, you can't turn your back on it.

The Challenge

Choose at least three married couples that you can tell this week, "marriage is a garden, dig it". If they ask you what you mean, explain it to them. Evaluate the way you manage the time spent with your spouse. Make sure you are spending intimate quality time with them on a regular basis. Pray that God will guide you on the steps to make your marriage a beautiful place to walk in together and that you keep the motivation to make it beautiful.

11. Say What?

Have you ever said something to your spouse that you wish you could take back? Have you ever wanted to say curse words that were on the tip of your tongue and you held back? We have all been there. Some of us may have taken it way too far. Our tongues have a way of getting us into a lot of trouble. James is pretty famous for talking about the tongue. In James 3:5 it says, "Even so the tongue is a little member and boasts great things. Behold, how great a matter a little fire kindles." Sometimes what we say goes much further than we intended. Have you ever begun an argument with your spouse to see it get way out of control? When we look back on our arguments, we can usually see a poor choice of words that was fuel on the fire. How great a matter a little fire kindles. Let's look at this from another angle. Are you in a marriage that is ok with the use of toxic and bad language? Do you casually use words to describe your spouse that does not honor them? Let's say that when you tell your friends something that your spouse did or said you are always calling them stupid or crazy. This can become part of the norm about the way you reference your spouse. Nothing good comes from this type of behavior. The thing is, the more you say it, the more it becomes part of your reality. But you say, it is reality. He really is stupid. She really is crazy. Well, you married them. That's on you. What you are supposed to do now is honor your spouse and develop behaviors that will encourage your marriage to get better. Let's go back to Sunday school when we were little. Treat others as you want to be treated. Wow, you mean I have to apply that to marriage too? If you want a good one. Do you want your spouse to say sweet things to you? Say sweet things to them. Do you want your spouse to speak well of you to others? Speak well of them to others. Do you want your spouse not to call you names? Don't call them names. Before you speak, think and say, is what I'm about to say going to be destructive to my spouse and my marriage? Sometimes we simply keep talking when it's time to stop. Proverbs 29:11 says, "A fool utters all his mind: but a wise man keeps it in till afterwards." Sometimes we need to calm down before we speak. Sometimes we need to stop speaking when we are losing our calm. Once the words leave our mouths, we can't take them back. Choose your words wisely.

The Challenge

Discuss words with your spouse that you use that maybe you shouldn't. Make an agreement to refrain from bad language and hurtful words. Commit to using words that build up and encourage each other. Pray and ask God to help you control what you say when you're with your spouse and when you're not.

12. Learn To Loose

Does anyone like losing? Winning is far more rewarding. The reality is however, losing is a normal part of life. As a parent with kids who play sports, I have tried very hard to help my kids win. I wish they could win every time. But what I have learned is that even more important than helping them win, I must help them learn how to lose. What they do when they lose will determine their next move. We all want wins in our marriages, but the reality is that we will go through times of loss. Sometimes, despite all our efforts, we seem to lose. But it's what we do after the loss that will determine our next move. In Philippians 4:12-13 Paul talks about things he has learned following Christ. He says, "I know how to be abased, and I know how to abound. Everywhere and in all things, I have learned both to be full and to be hungry, both to abound and to suffer need. I can do all things through Christ who strengthens me." The last part of that scripture is quoted a lot. I can do all things through Christ who strengthens me. People usually use that scripture to encourage themselves or others to accomplish a task or goal. It can absolutely be used that way. But Paul not only has this mindset when he is winning. He also has it when he is losing. Perhaps that is when he needs it the most. He points to his suffering. I know how to be abased, to be hungry, and to suffer need.

He knows how to go through these things and keep moving. He knows how to pick up the bat and step back up to the plate. It's Christ who gives him this strength. Does Christ give you this strength? I love to see married couples who have gone through great struggles and still love and care for each other. I see it as a great testimony to the power of a God blessed marriage. Sometimes we simply lose an argument. Sometimes we lose when having to make a decision. It is a common saying in our culture of marriage today that a woman is never wrong. If that is the case with your marriage than you may want to think about changing it up a little. If the woman always wins and the guy always loses, then there is not much incentive for him to play the game. Who wants to be in a marriage where all you know is defeat? If all we know is defeat as Christians, then the Christian life would be a pretty terrible one.

Thank God for all the victories He lets us experience through Him. Let your spouse experience some victories through you. When you both lose, pick yourselves up and get back to work.

The Challenge

Pick a card game or fast playing board game and play a couple rounds. Every time the game is over the loser has to tell the winner one thing they love about them. If one of you keeps winning, then reread the devotion. Pray that God helps your spouse win at life and at marriage.

13. That's Random

One thing among many that I admire about Jesus and the life He lived on earth was how random He was. He was different. Different than anyone who ever lived. He shocked the men at a young age with how much wisdom He had. He was unlike all the other spiritual leaders of that day, and most of them despised Him because of it. His miracles certainly set Him apart. People were drawn to Him just to see what He would say or do next. How random of a person are you? How random are you when it comes to your marriage? Do you ever do anything that catches your spouse off guard? Anything good I should say. Sometimes our marriages become way too predictable. This is absolutely a natural thing. The more time you spend with your spouse and the better you know each other, the more predictable your marriage will become. Predictable is also a good thing. But when it's too predictable, it has the threat of becoming boring. Early on in a relationship, people will go out of their way to do random things. If you really like the person, you try to get their attention in special ways. It's a mistake to stop this behavior just because you have some years under your belt. In the book of Ecclesiastes 1:9, Solomon talks a little about life. He says, "The thing that has been, it is that which shall be; and that which is done is that which shall be done: and there is no new thing under the sun." When you read this verse and the verses around it you can feel Solomon's frustration. In all his wisdom and all his wealth, he could not change the way life works. He had gained no more advantage over life than anyone else. We are all subject to the same life. Have you ever experienced this kind of frustration? We all know the same pitfalls and frustrations that marriage can bring. Frustration makes you say, 'there is no new thing under the sun'. Or you may say, 'this marriage will never change; it will always be like this.' Why don't you do something random and change it for the better. Be prepared to try something new. Be prepared to say something new. Some people get so bent out of shape that a simple, I love you, becomes difficult. It's a sad thing when you have become so confined that you can't perform a simple, random and loving act toward your spouse. Make an effort to catch your spouse off guard. Do something random that will turn their head. Don't get frustrated; get random.

The Challenge

Do something normal. Wait, you're already doing that. Do something random. Think hard and act on a good surprise for your spouse. Visit a new place. Surprise them at work. Go on a lunch date. Send them a series of loving texts. Detail their car for them. Come up with your own and do it. Pray that God will keep you from becoming frustrated and that He will inspire you to cultivate new life into your marriage.

14. Absence Makes The Heart Grow Peaceful

I wish I had learned this one early on in my marriage. Just because you are married doesn't mean you don't need your space. Especially when you are not seeing eye to eye. I used to think, if there was problem, I needed to fix it quickly and walking away was going to be detrimental to my marriage. This attitude led me to a lot of unnecessary anger. Let's look at Ephesians 4:26. It says, "Be angry and do not sin: do not let the sun go down on your wrath." At first glance we could gather that we should work out the problem so that the problem does not exist tomorrow. But let's really look at what its saying. Don't let the sun go down on your wrath. Your wrath and anger are what needs to be controlled. Sometimes the only way to control it is to get away from your spouse. I don't want you to leave the house every time you argue. That would not be productive.

But when tensions are getting high and anger is intensifying, a little space may do you both some good. Be angry and sin not. When your anger reaches an unhealthy place, you need to step back. Sometimes we get caught up in the heat of the moment and end up saying a lot of things that we didn't intend to say. A little space can help us reboot, gather our thoughts and revisit the disagreement with a rational mindset. I believe Solomon would have agreed with me on this one. He had many wives and I'm sure at times they were hard to get space from. In Proverbs 25:24 it reads, "It is better to dwell in the corner of a housetop, than with a brawling woman and in a wide house." I believe he is speaking from personal experience.

It's probably safe to say that a brawling woman has reached an unhealthy place on the anger scale. He says in another Proverb that it's better to dwell in the wilderness. If the house isn't big enough, you may have to venture a little further. Work out your problems. Don't leave them bottled up and undealt with. Just be careful that the sun doesn't go down upon your wrath. Space is a healthy thing when you are getting along and when you aren't. You certainly don't want personal space to only be applied when things aren't going so well. It's ok to have an adventure without your spouse. It gives you a good story to tell when you get back together. If you do have a problem and it doesn't get worked out today, that's ok. Just be diligent to keep a healthy attitude and a loving heart toward your spouse.

The Challenge

Make an agreement with your spouse that you will not allow your anger to get out of control. Allow one another to walk away so anger does not become sin. If you don't normally spend time apart, plan a separate adventure. Get back together later and share it with one another. Pray that God will reveal to you when anger has gone too far. Pray that your marriage finds peace, wherever it is.

15. Thank You

As I grew up, I had a mother and a grandmother that constantly corrected me as I responded to them and others. Yes ma'am and yes sir were pressed upon me greatly as well as being thankful. They wanted me to develop a polite attitude when dealing with people. I have noticed that people respond to you differently when you are polite. A simple thank you can go a long way. Are you polite to your spouse? Do you have a habit of saying thank you? Did you know that it is God's will that you make this a habit? In Paul's first letter to the Thessalonians he gives us some simple instructions. 1 Thessalonians 5:18 reads, "In everything give thanks: for this is the will of God in Christ Jesus concerning you." What's the will of God for your life? Have you ever wondered about that? I have wondered about that a great deal in my own life. Paul claims it's very simple. That you be thankful. You can't worship God with an unthankful attitude. Being thankful to God for all He has done for us changes our whole world. We look at life much differently. Most of the bible's instructions about daily living are about dealing with people. On your Job; in the store; in your own home; you have to deal with people. Just like Grandmaw, Paul is teaching us the power of a polite and thankful attitude. Jesus taught us to be motivated by love when we are dealing with people. We are supposed to love each other. All of us. Have you ever noticed that it is hard to be hateful and thankful at the same time? We can turn anything into a habit. We can come home every day and argue with our spouse because we have turned it into a habit. We can go to work every day with a negative attitude because we have turned it into a habit. In everything give thanks. Develop a habit of being thankful. Imagine how differently some of your conversations would go if you had a thankful attitude. Don't be that couple that is constantly hateful to one another. If your marriage isn't like that, then you probably know one that is. Couples get stuck in these ruts. Getting out of them could be as easy as, thank you. So, say thank you, a lot. Make it a habit. This does not guarantee that all our conversations will go smoothly. It does however give us a greater chance of success. When your feet hit the floor in the morning; be thankful. When you go to work; be thankful. When you eat; be thankful. When you look at your spouse; be thankful. This is God's will concerning you.

The Challenge

Every time you begin a conversation with your spouse say the words "thank you" before you say anything else. Try to do this for several days. Go a whole week if you can. Pray that God will reveal to you everything you have to be thankful for. Pray and thank God for your spouse. Make that prayer a habit.

16. Freedom In The Bedroom

Freedom is a word I believe everyone likes. We all want freedom in every aspects of our lives, especially within our marriages. Adam and Eve experienced a lot of freedom early on in their relationship. Before sin developed in their hearts, they were naked and unashamed. It wasn't until their spiritual fall that they began to be ashamed of one another. This is not what God intended marriage to be. To be completely free and unashamed with your spouse is at the height on marital bliss. Was it not this way early on in your relationship? Marriages usually start out with much freedom and acceptance as it should. But the difficult task in most marriages is to keep this freedom and build upon it. The marital bed should exercise this kind of freedom. In the book of Hebrews 13:4 it reads, "Marriage is honorable in all, and the bed undefiled: but whoremongers and adulterers God will judge." Marriage is honorable. It is a covenant created by God and is continually honored by God. As a result of this, the bed is undefiled. This is a statement of sexual freedom and it has Gods full support. God will however judge those acts of sexual fulfilment performed outside of the marriage covenant. Shame is rightly placed upon those who are acting in sin. But does this kind of shame belong in your marriage? If it's there, then you need to evaluate yourself. What is holding you back from being unashamed and free with your spouse? Usually if there are problems in the bedroom, they didn't start there. I praise God that we have spiritual freedom bought and paid for by Christ. In the gospel of John 8:36 it reads, "If the son therefore shall make you free, ye shall be free indeed." Of course, Jesus is not talking about sex specifically in this verse, but He is referring to your spiritual condition. What we must understand is that our spiritual and physical lives move together. When Adam and Eve disobeyed God, everything fell. Their spirit, their flesh and the world around them fell. Let the freedom you know in Christ motivate you to experience freedom in all aspects of your life. There is little doubt that you desire freedom with your spouse. To share your lives with one another without judgement. Honor your marriage and let the bedroom become a place a freedom; naked and unashamed.

The Challenge

Meet your spouse in the bedroom and you guessed it, be free. After you have experienced enough freedom pray that God will help you remove shame from your marriage. Pray for your spouse that they would know the spiritual freedom Jesus talked about in John 8:36.

17. Microscopic

Have you ever heard the saying; God is just as big in a microscope as He is in a telescope? Creation is an amazing thing. It testifies to the greatness and power of God. God did not only created a universe, with all its stars and planets and galaxies. He also created the microscopic elements and organisms that we can't see in the world all around us. God is a God of great detail. Have you ever done something big for your spouse? Perhaps you threw a big party or bought them something expensive. Maybe you planned a grand vacation. These things have the potential to better your marriage but the greatest acts you can perform are the small ones. These are the daily acts. The little things we do that make each other feel special and loved. Jesus gives us some insight in the gospel of Luke about the small things in our lives that He pays attention to. Luke 12:6-7 reads, "Are not five sparrows sold for two copper coins? And not one of them is forgotten before God. But the very hairs of your head are all numbered. Do not fear therefore; you are of more value than many sparrows." Can't you feel the intimacy in those verses? Can't you feel the security? Jesus lets us know how much He cares by showing us how well He knows us. He knows you. He pays attention to the details of your life. He wants you to know how much worth He sees in you. This should make you feel special. It sure makes me feel that way. Can't we apply this behavior inside our own homes? How do we do this? We have to get out the microscopes. Do you know how many hairs are on your spouse's head? Of course, you don't; unless your spouse is bald or close to it. But do you notice when they are sad or excited? Do you notice when they get their hair cut or when they lose a few pounds? Do you know if things are going well on their job or with their friends? Do you know if they think your marriage is in a good place? Didn't you have the microscope out when you started dating? Weren't you trying to figure out what they liked and didn't like? But you may say, I know everything about this person. It's not all about knowing them. It's about the way we speak and treat each other. Only part of the equation is paying attention to the small things. The other part is doing the small things. The little things, good or bad, add up to make your marriage what it is. Make your marriage as special on a Tuesday afternoon as it is on Saturday night. Make your marriage just as special when it's just the two of you as it is when you're surrounded by other couples. The earlier verse stated that "not one of them is forgotten before God." Don't forget about the small things and your spouse will not feel forgotten.

The Challenge

Look at or think about your spouse and write down as many details about them as you can. Really challenge yourself to see how many things you can write. Pray and ask God to help you see your spouse as He does. Thank God for the small things on your list that make your spouse who they are.

18. That Time Of The Month

Nobody likes that time of the month. Women and men both have to deal with it. It affects every marriage and can produce a lot of stress and frustration. Sometimes it rears its head at the worst times. It's that time of the month when all the bills are due. It hurts to see money come out of the bank account. It especially hurts when it's all your money. Four out of five families are living paycheck to paycheck. Can this add a great deal of stress to a marriage? We have a culture today that has normalized being in debt. It's just another part of everyday living. You're supposed to have a car payment, right? You need a credit card, don't you? It's almost as if we have been programmed to be in debt our entire lives. Proverbs 22:7 says, "The rich rules over the poor, and the borrower is servant to the lender."

The bible gives us a harsh reality that most of us don't want to face. We don't want to own up to the cost our debt plays on our lives and on our marriages. We say things like, "so and so has way more debt than we do", or "we work hard, we deserve this." We don't feel like slaves until we feel the pressure of the lender. We don't feel broke until we have $5 left in the account and our gas light is on. Have you ever had an argument about money in your marriage?

It's one of the leading causes of divorce, if you didn't know. Do you have your spending under control? Are you living within your means? Are you one of those couples that have your own money and your own debt? If you're going to be married, then you need to be married in every part of your lives. For richer or poorer right? Your wealth, my wealth. Your debt, my debt. We are in this thing together. Don't dump all the responsibilities of your bills and budget on your spouse. Work as a team and get it right. Our culture convinces us that debt is a blessing. The car dealers and the banks are doing us favors. Do yourself a favor and live within your means. The more debt you have, the more like a slave you will feel. The bank should not be your provider. The car salesman should not be your hero. Let the Lord be your provider and your hero. Let's leave room for God to show Himself strong in our finances. Philippians 4:19 says, "And my God shall supply all your need according to His riches in glory by Christ Jesus." What does your marriage rely on when it comes to money? Let it be Jesus.

The Challenge

Work on a budget if you don't have one. Work on a plan to get out of debt if you don't have one. There are many Christian programs that will help you. Dave Ramsey has a great one. Pray that God will give you the ability to see debt like He does and give your marriage the blessing of financial peace.

19. Live, Laugh, Stay Married

If marriage was no fun, I wouldn't want to do it. Maybe that's a simple reason people are choosing not to do it. Those that are not married may look at society's view of marriage as boring and a constant struggle. They may choose to not get married or just put it off. People that are married quit because it's not fun anymore. Isn't it sad to see couples that have been married for a long-time struggle? I can't help but think, why haven't they got this figured out yet? Whether they never laughed or forgot how to laugh it's evident that they have an anti-fun marriage.

Life is too short to be so miserable. I hope you would agree with me. Now marriage has its ups and downs. It's not always fun. But if it's hardly ever fun, then that's a real problem. Solomon talks in the book of Ecclesiastes; about the seasons we go through in life. Ecclesiastes 3:4 says, "A time to weep, and a time to laugh; a time to mourn, and a time to dance." In this verse and the verses around it, the writer is listing many of the changes we will see as we go through life. These are normal changes. No matter how hard you try, you will enter into a season of weeping at some point. This can be directly tied to your marriage. There will be seasons of weeping and mourning. But this shouldn't be the only season your marriage goes through. I don't mind a little bit of cold weather, but when I experience too much of it, I really start looking forward to the next season. I'm ready for some sunshine. Are you ready for some sunshine in your marriage? The good news is that you don't have to wait and see if a groundhog sees its shadow. You make the call as to what season you're going into next. I know that life will throw us curve balls we didn't anticipate that can really knock us off track. But we must have a mind that is made up. It's time to laugh.

It's time to dance. It's time to have some fun. Proverbs 17:22 reads, "A merry heart does good like a medicine: but a broken spirit dries the bones." A broken spirit sucks all the life out of the bones. This broken spirit within your marriage will do the same thing. Oh, but what can a merry heart do? It brings healing and life. Jesus came that we may have life, and that we may have it more abundantly as the Gospel of John puts it. I want everything Jesus is offering me. I want life. I also want the abundant part. I don't just want a marriage. I want the abundant part too. I hope you are living in its abundance. If you are, hang onto it. If you are not, then go and get it. It's within your reach. Live, laugh and stay married.

The Challenge

This one is simple; have fun. Make it a priority. Laugh till it hurts, then laugh some more. Pray that God fills your hearts with laughter and joy. Pray for His healing hand on any part of your marriage that is broken.

20. Your Feet Smell Good

Do you like your spouse's feet? Is that a weird question? You don't have to like your spouse's feet to get something out of this lesson; you just have to care about them. The same night as the last supper, Jesus did something none of His disciples expected. He got a pot of water and a towel and washed every one of His disciples' feet. I don't know how much Jesus actually liked feet, but He didn't wash them because it was fun. Let's look at why He did it. In John 13:4-5 it reads, "He rose from supper and laid aside His garments, took a towel and girded Himself. After that, He poured water into a basin and began to wash the disciple's feet, and to wipe them with the towel with which He was girded." Don't think I am going to simply tell you to go wash your spouse's feet. Jesus didn't teach them this practice because they had dirty feet. One reason Jesus did this was to show that He cared for them. The church according to scripture is the bride of Christ. He cares for His bride. Do you think He did a good job cleaning their feet? I think He washed them until they were clean. I want you to not only care about your spouse and serve them; but I want you to do it until the job is done. See it through until you see the results of your labor. If you serve your spouse just enough to get by, then you are losing out on a lot of fruitful results. If you aren't serving your spouse at all, then you are just plain losing. He tells them in John 13:15, "For I have given you an example, that you should do as I have done to you." He taught them this lesson because He wanted them to succeed. He was going to be killed. Things were going to change. He knew that if His church was going to grow and thrive, they would have to serve one another. Is this not true of marriage? Is your marriage growing and thriving? They were going to have to look out for each other and meet each other's needs. Jesus wanted them to do it well. He wants you to do it well too. He wants your marriage to be the kind of marriage He designed it to be. Jesus laid aside His own garments before He began washing their feet. Your own garments will have to be laid aside every once in a while, in order to serve your spouse. You may have to lay aside your feelings, wants and even comforts to serve them. He made a promise to them if they could understand this principle. John 13:17 says, "If you know these things, blessed are you if you do them." Lay aside your pride and become a blessing to your spouse. Get the water bucket out and get busy. Follow His example. Follow it well.

The Challenge

If you don't like feet this may be a hard challenge for you but do it anyway. Take turns and message each other's feet for at least 5 minutes. Do a good job too. Men; try to stay focused on just her feet. Pray that God will continually teach you about the lesson Jesus taught His disciples that day and how to apply it to your marriage.

21. Tipping The Scales

Have you ever wondered why your marriage or others around you struggle when you or others have the best of intentions? Sometimes things just aren't going well, and we don't understand why. One simple explanation could be a lack of balance. We have to balance everything in life. We give our jobs, our friends, our spouse, our children, our church, our hobbies an allotted amount of time, resources and energy. We do our best to balance these things in an effort to have a prosperous life. In an effort to balance everything, we can have the temptation to not give an area of our lives the attention it deserves. When one thing gets out of balance, the scales start tipping and it affects everything. Your marriage requires a lot of attention; attention that many people neglect. God likes balance. He believes in us having priorities in life. Matthew 6:33 says, "But seek ye first the kingdom of God, and His righteousness; and all these things shall be added unto you." God will not bestow blessings on our lives when we neglect to put Him first. He knows that what He blesses us with has to be balanced upon our faith in Him. Could that be a reason your marriage isn't being blessed? Put your marriage on the scales and see how it lines up with the word of God. Does your spouse get the love you promised them? Does your spouse get the friendship and support you promised them? Something as simple as you are working too much or watching too much TV can mess up the scales. It is sad that many people in our culture spend more time with their phone then they do with their spouse. So many things stem off of our marriages. If we can get the scales lining up in our marriages, many of the other things will fall into place. God should be number one. After that, your spouse should be your next priority. "A false balance is abomination to the Lord: but a just weight is His delight." That is Proverbs 11:1. The first step in making sure you have a balanced marriage is being honest about the weight you have put on the scales. Don't act like you do everything perfect and your spouse is the one who is failing. Look at the quality time you give your spouse. Look at the money and resources you put into your marriage. Not your stuff. I know you spend money and resources on stuff, as we all do. But right now, we are focusing on your relationship. What kind of energy and passion do you give your spouse? A just weight is the Lord's delight. Bring balance into your marriage and watch as God delights over you.

The Challenge

Have an honest discussion about the different areas in your lives that get your attention. Take an honest look at yourself and evaluate exactly what you are putting on the scales in your marriage. Pray that God gives you guidance on having a balanced marriage and a balanced life.

22. Take Pride In Me

In today's culture we have made it very normal for spouses to look down on each other. It's almost as if people's go-to, when asked about their spouse is some form of complaint. Friends get together and have a spouse bashing party. One person brings up something their husband or wife did, and everyone chimes in. You know that's true.

How many times have you gotten around a group of people and they were all talking about how wonderful their spouses were? We need to change this toxic environment.

We need to change it in our homes. If you knew your spouse was talking about you to someone; do you believe they would be taking pride in you, or putting you down? We have to learn and make it a constant habit to take pride in each other. Let's look at an example of taking pride in something from Romans 1:16. Paul says, "For I am not ashamed of the gospel of Christ: for it is the power of God to salvation for everyone who believes, for the Jew first and also for the Greek." I am sure there were many opportunities for Paul to put the gospel down. I'm sure that he was faced with many people that did. But he refused to join their foolishness. He had a great amount of pride in the gospel. He understood and appreciated what it meant to him and to God. Do you know how special your marriage is to God? Just like the gospel and its covenant belong to

Him, so does the covenant of marriage. When we take pride over our spouse, it reflects upon God. This is a part of your character and mindset I'm talking about. Of course, your spouse is going to do something stupid that you won't be proud of. However our go-to, in normal conversation should not be the stupidity of our spouse. We should be quick to lift them up, and extremely hesitant to put them down. Remember when you were a kid and you had that best friend? You would have done anything for them. If they were in a fight you would have had their back. If someone was putting them down, you would have stood up for them. Your mature marriage should far exceed the pride of a child. Take pride in them when everyone is watching, and when everyone is not. Take pride in them when they are struggling and when they are thriving. Take pride in them, knowing it honors God. How much would it change our culture and give people hope if we would all perfect this principle? Stop the shame and take pride.

The Challenge

Look for opportunities with people this week and start a conversation about marriage. Make it a point to say a few positive things about your spouse to them. Refuse the temptation to highlight anything negative, no matter what the other person says. Continually practice this principle and pray that God will remind you every day to take pride in your spouse.

23. Write The Vision

How many times have you taken a trip to somewhere far away that you had never been to, and didn't map it out? Did you just drive a direction hoping you would see signs and get lucky? That may work for a ten-minute drive. It's not going to work when you have to drive a day or two. Marriage is not a short journey. We have a long way to go; and it's going to take a long time to get there. We should set goals for everything we do in life. However, many people don't take the time to set goals for their marriages. If you don't have clear objectives; how will you know if you are going the right way? How will you know your reaching your correct destination? The Lord speaks to Habakkuk and tells him what to do for the people who by faith wait for Him to take action. Habakkuk needed guidance and that is what the Lord gave him. In Habakkuk 2:2 it reads, "Then the Lord answered me and said: Write the vision and make it plain on tablets, that he may run who reads it." I didn't know they had tablets back then; ha-ha. Write the vision. Write down the goals. Make them clear and easily understood. You may say; marriage isn't that complicated; we can just wing it. After all, if we just keep loving each other it will work out, right? Maybe you will get lucky and find your destination without ever looking at the map. But that's not likely. Goals not only keep you on a solid track together, but they also show you a clear destination. Do you both want the same thing in 5 years? Where do you see yourself in 15 years? Vision brings a level of excitement and energy into a marriage as well. When you both set a clear goal to pay off debt, you will be more motivated to accomplish it. When you both set a clear goal as to where you want to live; how you want your careers to advance; the ways you should discipline your children; you become each other's cheerleaders along the way. You will not only know the vision; you will run with it. If you fail to prepare, you must be prepared to fail. Your marriage has too much potential to just leave it to chance. When I was a teenager, I swam on a swim team. We swam in a 25-meter length pool. There were a lot of swimmers in the pool at one time. How did we stay in our lane? At the bottom of the pool there are straight lines that lead you clear across to the other side. If these lines were not there, we would have all swam in circles. How many marriages just keep going in circles? How many quit after 5 years, 10 years, or even 30 years. A solid vision will bring motivation and enthusiasm now and will provide much security for later in the marriage. Map it out and run with it.

The Challenge

Write the vision. Seriously write it down. Write some solid goals for your marriage. Think about money, church, where you live, your career, retirement, and children. Pray that you both become unified in your vision and that God will share His vision for your marriage with you.

24. Limits

It is incredible the amount of freedom marriage brings into our lives. The ability to not only share each other physically, emotionally, financially, and spiritually but to also have God's support along the way. This freedom has a way of removing many of our relational limits, but it does not remove them all. Sometimes we overstep our bounds and end up paying a price. The first year of my marriage, Brandy and I learned a great deal about each other. One morning she was in the bathroom curling her hair and I kept coming in and messing with her. I knew I was getting on her nerves, so it made me mess with her more. She threatened to hit me with the curling iron if I didn't leave her alone. I ignored her comment and kept bugging her. I thought; "there is no way she would hit me with a hot curling iron". As I was behind her, she threw her arm back and hit me in the inner bicep with her curling iron. I responded, "You burned me." She responded, "I told you I was going to." I learned a very important lesson that day. Marriage has its limits. I had a scar where I was burned for a solid year that reminded me of the lesson I had learned. As husbands and wives, we get pretty good at testing and pushing each other's limits. We need to be intentional about learning these limits and minding them. Solomon teaches us about the importance of time and how it can change on us drastically. In Ecclesiastes 3:4 and 7 it says, "A time to weep, and a time to laugh; a time to mourn, and a time to dance. A time to rend, and a time to sew; a time to keep silent, and a time to speak". We would do well to recognize the signs of the times in our marriages. There are times we need to push harder and there are times we need to back off. There are times we need to give advice and there are times we need to keep our mouths shut. Can I get an Amen! Learn these limitations and support each other through them. Don't try to dance with your spouse when they need a shoulder to cry on. Don't be distant when they need someone to talk to. Don't bug your wife while she has a very hot curling iron in her hand. Be a friend when a friend is needed. Be a lover when a lover is needed. There are plenty of things we deal with on a daily basis that push us to our limits. Our marriages should not be one of those things. Learn what makes each other thrive. Learn what makes your spouse light up and get excited and do those things. Stop pushing the limits. They will eventually push back.

The Challenge

Think about and talk about times you pushed the limits with your spouse. Recognize and point out any limits you currently are getting close to. Pray for freedom in your marriage and pray that God would teach you how to recognize whatever your spouse is going through and how to help them.

25. Tag You're It

Did you ever get all the neighborhood kids together when you were little and play tag? Everybody could join in on a game of tag. Tag, you're it. Being "it" was very tiring, especially when you couldn't catch anyone. I remember kids just giving up because they were tired of running and never tagging anyone. They were no longer having fun at that point. Tag was a fun, healthy game that got a lot of our unused energy out. The marriage relationship can sometimes feel like a game of tag, especially when it comes to sex. There is usually one person in the relationship that is running and the other one is chasing. The men are usually the ones chasing their wife down for some physical activity. This can be a fun game between the husband and wife as long as there is an eventual "tag". The problem comes in when the runner never lets the chaser tag them. The chaser will eventually stop having fun and become disappointed and frustrated. The runner looks back and notices that their spouse is no longer playing the game. There is a physical and emotional distance between them now and it's unhealthy. The game is fun as long as everyone is playing. I don't care how long you have been married; you still need to play the game.

Paul speaks in 1 Corinthians about the physical relationship between a husband and wife. 1 Corinthians 7:4 reads, "The wife does not have authority over her own body, but the husband does. And likewise, the husband does not have authority over his own body, but the wife does." He is urging them to allow one another to play the game. Don't be stingy with your body. It is not your body anymore. Let's say, it's not only yours. Paul goes on to tell them that if they neglect each other physically, Satan can tempt the lack of control that the neglect creates. We definitely don't want to push each other toward temptation. This is why we need to take special care to connect physically as married couples on a regular basis. What a horrible affect it has on a marriage to take physical authority away from your spouse. Don't take this right away from one another. Take Paul's advice and empower each other. Sometimes the chaser needs to slow down and let the runner have a break. Sometime the runner needs to let the chaser catch up. However you play the game, make sure there is a balance you both find acceptable. Let the games begin. Tag, you're it.

The Challenge

Have a discussing and figure out if you both find the way you are playing the game acceptable. Are you both happy with your sex life? Give your spouse the authority to make changes if necessary. Create a balance you both find acceptable. Pray for each other and ask God to bless your sex life and keep you from temptation.

26. Remember

Are you a forgetful person? I believe most ladies would say that their husbands are pretty forgetful. If I can remember half the stuff my wife tells me then I'm doing well. We all struggle with forgetfulness. We set reminders on our phones. We tell Alexa things to remind us about. We write on sticky notes and put them on our fridge or dresser. This is a normal part of life. I don't believe any of you occasionally forget you are married; but you may occasionally forget why. The reality is, we need to be reminded of our why sometimes. Jesus, at the last supper, gave His disciples bread and wine. These things they ate and drank to symbolize His body and blood that would be sacrificed for their sins and ours. He told them to do this, "in remembrance of me." This can be found in the book of Luke 22:19. We have communion in our churches throughout the year to remind us of what Jesus did for us. Not that we forget it happened. We need reminded of the why. The day you got married you and your spouse gave each other a gift. This gift was given so that you would be identified as a married person. It was also given as a reminder of the other person that you have joined yourself to. It is the wedding ring. What a great tradition. I couldn't wait to put the ring on the hand of my wife. I gave Brandy her ring with the intention that she would wear it, "in remembrance of me." I hope you wear a wedding ring. I hope you wear it proudly. It doesn't matter if it's a $20 ring or a $5,000 ring as long as it does its job. When you are faced with a tough decision to make. When you are balancing the checkbook and figuring out how to pay the bills. When you have a terrifying medical diagnosis. When an attractive coworker hits on you. Even when we go through the motions of another routine day. These are the moments when we need to take our thumb and pinky and spin that ring around our finger and put ourselves in remembrance of our spouse. You didn't forget you were married. You may have forgotten your companion, your lover, your friend. I believe God loves reminders. When the water had receded after God had flooded the earth, He gave a sign in the sky. He created the rainbow. He put the rainbow in the sky as a reminder of the covenant He made with the earth and all its living creatures to never destroy it again by flood. Do you think God could really forget? Perhaps He just wanted something pretty to look at to remember His why. It is also for us to look at and remember the promise God gave us long ago. You are only half of your marriage. There is another half; a better half. Spin that ring around and remember them.

The Challenge

Go get your wedding ring if you don't have it. Reenact the scene of you giving it to your spouse on your wedding day. Talk about what it meant to you that day. Remember the why. Pray that God will put reminders in your path to better remember your spouse. Remember and thank God for what He has done for you.

27. Good Hurt

Have you ever been to the gym and pushed yourself hard with a workout? I hope you work out on some level. We need to look good for our spouses. Nobody wants to be married to a couch potato. After that hard workout your muscles got really sore. Sometimes that soreness can last for days. I call this kind of pain a good hurt. It lets you know you did a good job stretching those muscles, which causes them to grow. You will do one of two things after you have experienced this pain. You will quit working out or you will get back to it. Anything that will better you, will hurt on some level. It will require some type of sacrifice. Marriage is no exception. Marriage is going to hurt sometimes. Sometimes it's supposed to. Your boss at work should challenge you in order to get the best out of you. Your Pastor at church should challenge you to be the greatest child of God you can be. Do you not think your marriage should challenge you in the same kind of ways? I believed God designed marriage to do just that. Can your muscles really grow without you pushing them past comfort? You don't quit when it hurts. You push passed it, knowing you will come out better on the other side. We are told over and over in the bible that being a Christian comes with a lot of challenges. 1 Peter 1:7 reads, "That the trial of your faith, being much more precious than gold that perisheth, though it be tried with fire, might be found unto praise and honor and glory at the appearing of Jesus Christ." Our faith will be tried and tested the same way gold is refined; through fire. But Peter encourages us to see these trials as a good hurt. Not that they feel good, but what it pushes us toward is praise, honor, and glory in our God. If you work out on a regular basis, then you know the pain is a temporary discomfort to a great result. You even begin to challenge yourself harder and harder. Use your marriage to grow and become a better you. Get it through your head that your spouse is supposed to challenge you. My marriage certainly challenges me. Brandy and I are very different people. Not in the since of our morals and beliefs. We are different when it comes to making decisions, handling conflict, spending money, disciplining our children and so on. These differences force us to stop and look at situations from another angle. I believe the way we challenge one another and our ability to compromise has yielded fantastic results. I would certainly do things much different on my own. I would definitely have less clothes that matched. Embrace your differences and accept the challenge. Don't quit when the hurt comes. It's a good hurt.

The Challenge

Have a discussion with your spouse about the ways you are different, or, you can take pen and paper and write some of these down. Think of ways these differences are good for you. Pray and thank God that your spouse is not just like you. Pray that He will teach you how to embrace these differences and use them to grow a stronger marriage.

28. Offense Vs. Defense

In many team sports you have the offence and the defense. The offence is trying to score while the defense is trying to keep the other team from scoring. This is a great balance when it comes to sports. It's not so great a balance when it comes to marriage. When we both play offensively in marriage, we are both trying to score and win. But when we both play the defense we never score and never get a win. Peter was an on-fire disciple that loved Jesus. He absolutely wanted to see Jesus win. He said in Luke 22:33 "I am ready to go with you, both to prison, and to death." I believe Peter was playing offence and went as far to say he would die for Jesus. But in Luke 22:56, after Jesus had been taken captive, a woman claimed that Peter was one of Christ's disciples. In verse 57 Peter responded to her and said, "woman I know him not." Wow, what happened? Peter got pretty defensive and actually ended up denying the Lord three times. Why this sudden change so quickly? Peter was the same guy he was just hours before but the circumstances that surrounded his relationship with Jesus changed dramatically. One thing about the circumstances of your marriage that is for certain, is that they will change. Some of these changes are brought on by having children, changing jobs, moving, financial success or financial burden. But we also just change as people. Our attitudes and outlooks on life change. We must be careful through whatever changes we go through not to go on the defense. Peter quickly forgot about his care for Jesus and began looking out for himself. We are defensive in our marriages sometimes because we are trying to protect ourselves. We say and do hurtful things in an effort to keep our spouse from winning. But marriage is not a football game. Stop emotionally tackling your spouse in an effort to make them lose. If your spouse loses, you lose too. If everyone would learn that simple principle, the marriages around us would look very differently. When you said, "I do", you made a promise to see your spouse through whatever comes your way. You promised to help them win in life. Don't let circumstances change this promise. You will win together, or you will lose together. Win.

The Challenge

Try your best to think of ways you have denied your spouse. Do you hold anything back from them in an effort to hurt them? Think about this; denying Jesus only made Peter's life more miserable. Are there things you do that only make your marriage more difficult and never help it? Commit to changing these habits and go on the offence. Pray that God will teach you how to play the offence and will give you a winning marriage.

29. Hold My Hand

Do you like holding hands with your spouse? I can't help but believe it is a very healthy thing for a married couple to do. I don't have an awesome statistic to show you that couples that hold hands are more likely to have a better marriage; although it probably exists somewhere. We will just have to look at it from a practical standpoint. Have you ever seen a married couple holding hands and arguing at the same time? I'm talking about the serious type of arguing. When things are not going well, or we begin to argue we tend to put distance between each other. Intimacy and fighting don't really mesh well together. But one of those things can prevent the other. If we keep fighting then we will by effect, diminish our intimacy. However, if we will increase our intimacy, we can lessen our likelihood of fighting. I know that some people are touchier than others. I am certainly a more physical person than my wife. Any marriage will benefit from non-sexual touching. Of course, it will benefit from sexual touching but that is not what we are talking about right now. Why is it powerful? It sends a message. It lets your spouse know that you are there with no strings attached. I'm not holding your hand because it will lead to sex or something else I want. I simply want to hold your hand. When we were children, we benefited a great deal from this type of physical touch. Mom or Dad would hug or kiss you just because they loved you. Momma would rock you to sleep at night. Daddy would pick you up off the ground and hold you after you fell. These little displays of physical contact give us comfort and security as children. They do the same as adults. Of course, it looks different. Your spouse is not going to rock you to sleep at night. That would be weird. But they can put your hand in theirs and give you the same amount of comfort and security. There is a story in the bible about the disciples being in a ship in the midst of the sea. Jesus walked to them on the water and they began to be afraid. After they realized it was Jesus, Peter requested that he be allowed to walk on the water with Jesus. Jesus told him to come. Peter began to be afraid and sink in the water. He cried out for Jesus to save Him. The first part of Matthew 14:31 says, "And immediately Jesus stretched forth His hand and caught him." How much security did Peter feel when Jesus grabbed his hand? It changed his fear into a teachable moment about the love Jesus had for him. This is an extreme example that shows a simple truth. When you hold your spouse's hand, you let them know, I'm right here. I am with you. I am for you. You don't have to wait on a scary situation to grab them by the hand. Hold their hand because you simply want to. You can always let go if you want to fight, but holding hands is healthier, and much safer.

The Challenge

In the car, on the couch, or walking into the store. All of these are great opportunities for you both to hold hands. Be more intentional this week about holding hands. Pray and ask God to add security to your marriage and to your walk with Him.

30. Empowered Leadership

It shouldn't be any surprise to the Christian couple that leadership plays an important role in marriage. It also shouldn't be a surprise that God has called the husband to lead his family. This does not mean a wife cannot be a leader or that she does not directly impact the future of her family. It does mean however that God has put a responsibility in the heart of a man that is specific to him. Ephesians 5:23 reads, "For the husband is the head of the wife, even as Christ is the head of the church: and He is the savior of the body." This is a great responsibility He has put on the husband. He cannot perform this responsibility without the support of his wife. Ladies; you have the ongoing ability to empower him to lead. Men; you have to be willing to lead. You have to step up and lead your family in the fear of the Lord. Ladies; you can help him accomplish this. There is one characteristic that makes someone a leader. They have to have a follower or followers. If you do not have a single follower, then you are not a leader. For this principle of scripture to be practiced correctly the man must lead his wife and the wife must follow her husband. How is this working in your marriage? You are not supposed to follow your husband because he is perfect. You don't just follow his lead when he does something right. Follow him because it is the most effective way to encourage him to lead. Do you want your husband to lead you? If you want the absolute best out of him then your answer should be yes. Men and women both have a major influence upon one another in a marriage. This influence can be used to build each other up or tear each other apart. In the book of 1 Timothy Paul shares some qualifications for Bishops in the church. In the 5th verse of chapter 3 it reads, "For if a man know not how to rule his own house, how shall he take care of the church of God?" He alludes to the fact that a man cannot lead in the church if he can't lead in his own home. I believe he will have a hard time leading anything if he can't lead in his own home. The respect he receives there will spill into every part of his life. Ladies; do you want your man to be successful at his job, at his church, and in his community? Encourage and empower him to be successful in his home. In order to do that, he must lead. Wife; push him to lead. Husband; give her something worth following. This is somewhat anti culture today. People believe this way of thinking is outdated. No matter how culture and times change, we are still built the same. The word of God has not changed. Ladies; empower your man to lead. You will be glad you did.

The Challenge

Men; give yourself an evaluation on the way you lead your family. Ladies; do an evaluation from your point of view about his leadership. Discuss your results and future expectations of his leadership. Men; pray over your wife and ask God to give you the wisdom and love to lead her. Ladies; ask God to give you patience toward your husband and to show you how to encourage him to lead.

31. Pillow Talk

Do you ever go to bed at the same time as your spouse? If you are going to have pillow talk, you both have to be in the bed at the same time and conscious. If Brandy is in the bed before me and I don't hurry up there will be no pillow talk. She is a nurse and she likes her sleep. I know we converse throughout the day, but pillow talk is different. By the time you lay down you have officially said, "This day is over". After you're done playing on your phone of course. Now it is just the two of you with nothing to do but sleep. This is a great time to have a short intimate conversation without distraction. It's also a great time to play tag but that's in another discussion. When we have 100 things going on, we can still have a conversation, but it's hard to make it intimate. We need to make sure we carve out time to truly get into some simple intimate conversation with our spouse. A relaxed conversation is the best kind. It's important, but don't take pillow talk to seriously. It needs to be fun. It needs to sometimes get goofy. It needs to be easy going and laid back. Seriously, you should have your head laid back on the pillow. This is not the time to share life changing information. Don't get mad at your spouse the next day when they forgot that thing you told them when they were half asleep. Pillow talk is more about connecting intimately with each other than it is about sharing information. If it is not reasonable that you can go to bed at the same time, then have this same type of conversation on the couch or on the front porch swing. Just make sure you still have a pillow. The pillow is vital. This will help pave the way for some great sleep. We can sleep well knowing that our marriage is being blessed. The bible tells us that a good relationship with the Lord will help our sleep as well. When we stay connected with Him, it gives us peace. Proverbs 3:24 reads, "When you lie down, you will not be afraid; yes, you will lie down, and your sleep will be sweet." Our connection with God provides this comfort. Your spouse will never be able to give you what God can. They can, however, bring you comfort and peace. They can help you get rid of your fears so your sleep can be sweet. Is your marriage that good? Is it better than any sleep medication a doctor can give you? Maybe it's time you're prescribed a little bit of pillow talk. Get under the covers, tangles those legs up and say something goofy.

The Challenge

This is an easy one. I understand not everyone can go to bed at the same time but try to if you can. Get some good simple pillow talk going. Get goofy and have fun. Pray that God will bless your conversations and use them to add intimacy to your marriage.

32. Irreconcilable Differences

Have you ever heard the phrase irreconcilable differences? It's a pretty common phrase in the divorce world. I hope and pray it is never a common phrase in your world. When a married couple wants a divorce, they must have a reason.

To state irreconcilable differences is to simply say, we can't get along. The definition states that their differences are beyond resolution. Every marriage has the potential to reach this level of destruction. On the other hand, every marriage has the potential to succeed. God does not expect us to have a marriage of irreconcilable differences, but a marriage of reconciliation. To reconcile simply means to restore. Jesus reconciled us to God through his death on the cross. In 2 Corinthians 5:18 it says, "Now all things are of God, who has reconciled us to Himself through Jesus Christ, and has given us the ministry of reconciliation." He has given us a ministry. He has given us a purpose and a calling. He has given us reconciliation. This is Gospel. This is great news. We are now called to pay it forward. What better way to pay it forward then with your spouse? I hope you have been restored to God through the blood of Jesus. If not, I hope you one day discover the salvation that can only be found in Him. You will not regret it. How often do you have a difference of opinion with someone? This principle of scripture is something we are supposed to practice with people every day. God has given us grace.

We are supposed to show grace to others. If you are married, then there is a good chance you and your spouse have some differing opinions. I have said it many times, that marriage is a great teacher. It teaches us about life and about God. Marriage should teach you how to deal with people. Marriage is a place we should learn how to resolve conflict, compromise and control our attitudes. It should testify of and display the Gospel. God has called us to help Him reconcile the world to Himself. We all have the potential to help Him with that. Let your marriage help teach you how to perfect a ministry of reconciliation. The differences we have should not be an opportunity for failure. They should be an opportunity to practice ministry. They should not be an opportunity to say you are beyond resolution; but an opportunity to stand resolute. Let your marriage be a shining example of what God can do. Let it testify of Him.

The Challenge

Break out the Bible and read 2 Corinthians chapter 5. This is very encouraging and inspiring scripture to the believer. Let it encourage and inspire your marriage. Pray that God will teach you how to practice reconciliation in your marriage in order to bring glory to him. Thank Him for restoring us to new life.

33. Slippery Slope

How quickly can you pick up speed when you are traveling downhill? Your car, your bike and even your legs will start moving faster. When it comes to marriage, certain behaviors can have a way of picking up speed and becoming a slippery slope. One of these behaviors is a negative attitude. Have you ever noticed how negative people are always negative? People get stuck there and have a hard time getting out. If we are not careful, our marriages can get stuck there as well. When you are dealing with your spouse, are you more prone to a positive response or a negative response? We use positive or negative reinforcement when it comes to disciplining a child or dog. I hope you don't treat your spouse like either of those, but we still respond to each other in these ways. We try to motivate one another toward a certain action or way of thinking. The problem with using a negative attitude with your spouse is that is breeds more and more negativity and leads to resentment. This type of behavior is not a motivator for me. Is it a motivator for you? This is an issue that the Author of Hebrews discusses in the 10th chapter. He's encouraging them to support one another as the church. Hebrews 10:24 reads, "And let us consider one another to provoke unto love and to good works." In your marriage, one way or another, you are going to provoke your spouse. Why not learn how to provoke them to love and good works? Learn the behaviors that yield positive and motivating results. Create an atmosphere your spouse wants to come home to. Really think about that one. Does your spouse think about you all day with an anticipation to see you? Does your spouse try to avoid any thought of you and dread coming home? Reread those last two sentences and be honest with yourself. Simple behaviors make all the difference on which one describes your spouse. Do you want a good marriage? Do you want your spouse to want you? Give them something positive to remember. Give them something rewarding they desire to come home to. Negativity is a downhill ride we need to put the brakes on. Positivity is an uphill climb; but boy is it worth it. Avoid the slippery slope of negativity. Some of you have been riding down that hill so long you believe it's the only way to go. It will rob you of a great marriage. It will rob you of joy. Love each other and treat each other with good works. It will lead to more good works and a stronger love.

The Challenge

Discuss any behaviors you find to be negative with the ways you treat each other. Think of and implement more positive and motivating behaviors. Pray that God will keep you from the cliff of negativity. Pray that He teaches you how to create an atmosphere of encouragement for your spouse.

34. Holy Perfection

Does the word perfect belong anywhere in your marriage? Do you believe there is such a thing as a perfect marriage? Stop thinking of that married couple you know that looks like they have it all figured out. Let's look within and challenge ourselves with what God thinks you're capable of. Does God expect perfection? There are a few bible verses that would make you assume He does. Matthew 5:48 says, "Be ye therefore perfect, even as your Father which is in heaven is perfect." I have no doubt that God is perfect. But does He really expect us to be? The word perfect used in the passage does not suggest that we can be just like God. God certainly knows we can't achieve that. The word is closely related to the idea of maturity. In the context of this bible verse Jesus is talking to them about love. He is telling them to love perfectly. To have a mature love. Would He tell us to be perfect if it were an impossibility? You will never be a perfect God, but you can be a perfect you. This is also true of marriage. Most people struggle with this concept. They see perfection as an attitude that holds us back and only brings judgement upon ourselves. Many people won't even try to better themselves as they say, "nobody's perfect." Don't use this as a cop out. Don't be that person who never owns up to their sins because, "he that is without sin should cast the first stone." Would you rather Jesus have said, don't even try because you can't do it. There is a world full of people that will tell you that. There are plenty of divorced people that will counsel you to get a divorce. No; He wants you to strive for something greater. He is not suggesting you will never struggle. He simply wants you to move forward; to press yourself into perfection. Stop making excuses why your marriage will never function right. Be perfect, as your

Father in heaven is perfect. Find out what the will of God is for your marriage and strive for it. Be your best self. Make your marriage its best self. Another verse is 1 Peter 1:16 and it reads, "Because it is written, Be ye holy; for I am holy." Holy means set apart. As Christians we are to be set apart to God. Normal in the world is lust, pride and wickedness. God desires that you be set apart from that. Normal marriage in the world is lust, pride and wickedness. Will you set your marriage apart from that? If a crappy marriage is normal, then it's time to be weird. There are plenty of people that are ok with you having a bad marriage. It makes them feel better about their terrible marriage. Make your marriage a head turner. Make it weird to the world. Move it closer and closer to holy perfection.

The Challenge

Make 2 lists on a piece of paper. In one column write the characteristics of a worldly marriage. In the other, write a list of characteristics that describe a holy and perfect marriage. Discuss which list your marriage mostly lines up with. Pray for one another and challenge each other to move on into perfection.

35. Spill Your Guts

Have you ever learned how to effectively and successfully communicate with your spouse? Note that I said effectively and successfully. It is no secret that communication is a key element in any successful marriage. Many married couples, new and old, struggle with communication. There are plenty of books and marriage seminars that revolve around this one challenge in marriages. I want to simply challenge you now to a good conversation. When you were dating, you tried your best to find out information about each other so you could learn and act appropriately. You wanted to find out what each other liked to do for fun so you could plan a fun activity. You wanted to find out what kind of food each other liked so you would make reservations at the right restaurant. You found out what kind of music each other liked so you would tune in to the right station. You also choose your words carefully as to impress your date. In 2 Corinthians chapter 6, Paul is speaking to them about the different things he goes through in ministry for their sakes. He speaks about the hardships, challenges, and victories. In 2 Corinthians 6:11 it reads, "O Corinthians! We have spoken openly to you, our heart is wide open." He lets them know that he has held nothing back and has poured out his heart unto them. Does your spouse believe that about you? Do they know about your hardships, challenges, and victories? If they don't, maybe it's time to tell them. One of the most important aspects of communication is the act of sharing information. You had to make all kinds of decisions while you dated. You collected information so you could make an informed decision. You can't make an informed decision without information. This is a simple reason a husband and wife can start growing apart. They stop sharing information. Never assume that you know each other so well that you no longer need to communicate like you once did. Never take it for granted when your spouse has something to share with you. Always be looking for information you can learn from. Have you ever seen that couple at the restaurant that looks like they have nothing to talk about? It's almost awkward. Did I just describe you and your spouse at the restaurant? We can get this way when we stop sharing information. We stop telling stories. We need to share our day and our experiences with each other. It should be a normal behavior. If it is not, then it will become awkward. Maybe it's time to have a good old fashion conversation. Share your hardships, challenges and victories. Tell a story. Spill your guts and have fun.

The Challenge

It's time to challenge each other to some new information. Try to come up with something new to share every day this week. Men; try not to zone out. Ladies; if you information overload him, his head will explode, so be careful. Ask God to continually teach you how to communicate well with each other.

36. Heaven

Will you still be married in heaven? Do you still want to be married in heaven? If you have a great marriage, then you probably do. If your marriage isn't going so well then you are probably looking forward to the death do us part. Hopefully that is not the only part of your wedding vows you remember. Jesus gives us some insight into this subject in the Gospel of Matthew. The Sadducees came up to Jesus and asked Him a question. They told Him of a woman who married the brother of her deceased husband. After that husband died, she married another brother. She did this seven times. They asked Jesus whose wife she will be in heaven. In Matthew 22:30 Jesus said, "For in the resurrection they neither marry, nor are given in marriage, but are as the angels of God in heaven." Based on these words we can make the conclusion that we will no longer be married in heaven. If marriage is not truly forever, then is it really that important? Should we quit wasting our time building a relationship that will one day end? Let's look at this from a few different angles. God said that it was not good for man to be alone. He created Eve and presented her to Adam as a helpmate. Why did God give him a helpmate? Because he needed one. You need one too. God built the family with the intention that they would help each other on this journey called life. In heaven, the atmosphere we live in will change. We will no longer live in a fallen world. It will no longer be necessary to have a helpmate making sure we get through it. God himself will be our helpmate. Your marriage should be helping you. It should be teaching you. It should be making you a stronger Christian. If not, then you're doing it wrong. Does this mean however that we won't understand we were husband and wife in heaven? Will we forget about our lives together? There is nothing in the bible that brings me to that conclusion. I challenge you to see heaven as a place of revelation, not a place of ignorance. You will not be ignorant about the sins you committed, the choices you made, or the relationships you had. You will have a greater understanding of these things. The small glimpses of heaven we get in scripture show us that people are still who they were. They are recognizable. They understand what is happening around them. I believe I will know Brandy in heaven. I believe we will remember the marriage we had. Our relationship will look different though. I have no doubt that it will be a good different. All of our eternity is built upon the foundations we make here. Your marriage is part of that foundation. Build a strong foundation. Let Jesus be its chief Cornerstone.

The Challenge

Talk about heaven and what it will be like. If you are clueless then look up some bible verses about heaven to help you. Discuss how your relationship may look in heaven. Pray that God will give you a great desire for heaven. Ask Him to bless the foundations of your faith and your marriage and make them strong.

37. Beautiful

Do you think your spouse is beautiful? I am not talking about inward beauty. I am talking about the outward appearance. Of course, beauty on the inside is far more important but let's talk briefly about what our eyes can see. Look at your spouse. Look at their eyes, their nose and their mouth. Look at their hair, their clothes and their feet. Are they beautiful? Attraction is powerful inside of a marriage. Yes, it was powerful when you first got together. You would not have dated someone you didn't find attractive. Attraction is what grabbed ahold of you and made you schedule the second date. Is attraction still important to you? Does attraction still grab ahold of you? As our marriages grow and mature, the way we look doesn't have the same impact. I have a lot less hair now then when Brandy and I dated. She is so in love with me now that it's not a big deal. It would have probably been a bigger deal on the first date. Maybe not a deal breaker for her, but a bigger deal. Of course, people that are 80 years old look far different than they once did. This does not mean however that attraction is no longer important. We need to look good for each other. We need to keep the attraction. Men; don't assume you can stop taking care of yourself because you got her locked in. Ladies; don't assume the sweatpants are all you need to wear because he doesn't care. Look nice for each other. Stay fit for each other. Be intentional about your spouse finding you attractive. The Song Of Solomon shares the love story of a man and a woman. It also relates to the love Christ has for His church. In Song of Solomon 4:1 and 3 it reads. "Behold, you are fair, my love! Behold, you are fair! You have dove's eyes behind your veil. Your hair is like a flock of goats, going down from Mount Gilead. Your lips are like a strand of scarlet, and your mouth is lovely. Your temples behind your veil are like a piece of pomegranate." Yes, the imagery used here is a little outdated. But you can still see his attention to detail. He is in love with her. He finds her extremely attractive. What a shame it is for a marriage to lose this powerful tool. If your marriage has lost it, or has let it fade, it's time to pick it back up. Do what Solomon's girl did. Fix your hair nice and brush your teeth. Make your hair like a flock of goats and your mouth lovely. Remember you are beautiful. If your spouse married you, then they must think you are. Keep the attraction going and show off your beauty.

The Challenge

Discuss what attracted you to each other when you first started dating. Discuss how that has changed and what you find attractive now. Make an intentional act this week of looking attractive for each other. Ask God to help you see the beauty inside and out that your spouse has.

38. The Old File Cabinet

If one of you in the marriage is an organized person than there is a good chance, there is a file cabinet of some sort in your home. Inside, all the bills are categorized. The birth certificates may be in there. Your old tax returns are filled by year. After a few years of marriage, the file cabinet can start getting a little heavy. It may be time to get it cleaned out. Those energy bill receipts from 5 years ago need to be tossed. The information on that car you no longer own can be trashed. Inside of every marriage there is an old file cabinet. Not a literal one like your bills are in; but a figurative one that holds glimpses into the past. We can go through periods of time when we never mess with this file cabinet and we can go through times where we access it daily. What we all have inside of our marriage is history. This looks different from marriage to marriage. Some marriages have a rough history with a lot of hurt and disappointments. Some have had minor setbacks that challenged the relationship. Everything we go through as a couple gets filled away. Is it time to get rid of some of that history? It's a great thing to remember where you came from. To look back and see what you have gone through together and made it. But the dangerous part about keeping the old file cabinet around is that it can be used as a weapon against each other. Have you ever been in an argument with your spouse and brought up something your spouse did in the past to support your argument? Have you ever reached way back in the file cabinet to pull something out from years ago? If you were in a street fight with your hands empty, you would quickly look for something you can pick up to either throw or use to strike your opponent. In marriage when an argument starts, we start looking for a weapon as well. This weapon is usually in the form of a past mistake. The past mistakes are found in that old file cabinet you carry around. The only thing that can help you clean out the old files is forgiveness. You will not have a successful marriage without forgiveness. You may claim that you forgave your spouse, but if you still have the files at your disposal, then you never really did. To forgive something means I won't hold this against you. Can you imagine going to heaven believing that you have had your sins forgiven only to see God pull out your file? How would it feel to have the Lord read out all your mistakes and hold them against you? I don't think any of us would make it in. Psalm 103:12 reads, "As far as the east is from the west, so far has He removed our transgressions from us." When God forgives, He lets it go. When you forgive your spouse, you need to let it go. One fact about the past is that it will never change. Don't hold it against each other. Clean out the old files and get focused on the new ones. Jesus made all things new, so can you.

The Challenge

Look at the old file cabinet. You can look at the literal one and the figurative one if you want. Figure out which files you need to throw out. Pray that God will teach you to forgive as He does. Ask God to reveal any old files that you use to hurt your spouse and ask Him to help you let them go.

39. Stuck Like Glue

At what point in your marriage did you realize you are stuck with this person? I remember Brandy telling me in the first year of our marriage that if she knew I was like this she would not have married me. She was joking, I think. Living with me was a little different than just being engaged to me. At what point did you realize you were stuck with this family you married into? That reality hits every man and every woman at some point. It usually doesn't take very long. In Laws can be a major point of frustration in a marriage. There is a natural separation that occurs when a man in woman join in marriage. Genesis 2:24 reads, "Therefore shall a man leave his father and mother, and shall cleave unto his wife: and they shall be one flesh." This is a simple, easy to read verse, but it can be very difficult to play out in your marriage. If we are supposed to turn from our blood family and focus on our spouse, then where do the in laws fit into our lives? The act of leaving and cleaving is played out in a few different ways. You are no longer dependent on your parents. You should be dependent on each other. You should work to support each other and your children if you have them. When you have to make a life choice, you don't call momma. When you're facing a struggle, you don't call daddy. Sure, you can always get their advice, but not without first seeking the advice of your spouse. This can be a major adjustment for a person, especially if they were very close to their parents. There is a new foundation that must be laid. What you now build in life should rise off of the foundation of your marriage. Let's say that you're in laws are the ones struggling with this. Let's say they are causing you to argue because of their actions and comments. Try not to turn this struggle against each other.

Ladies; don't make him disown his mother. Men; understand that she will always look up to her dad. The act of honoring your father and mother is never off the table. Let the past be in the past and move on. Forgive wrongdoing and focus on your marriage. Sometimes problems with in-laws never change. You can let it hurt your marriage for the rest of your lives or you can learn to live with it. Learn to live with it. Learn to live past it. Try not to put your spouse in a position where they have to choose you or their family. You should never be put in that position. Your marriage is too important to be put in such an ultimatum. Always make sure your spouse knows that they come first and can depend on you. Use your in-laws to practice patience. Love them no matter what. After all, you're stuck with them.

The Challenge

Each of you name a few reasons why you love your in-laws. Come on, you can do it. Talk about ways you can improve these relationships. If there is a present struggle that you're both facing, lay out a plan to live with it and move past it. Pray for your in-laws. Ask God to bless them.

40. Will You Trust Me?

Who wants a marriage that has no intimacy? I don't want to live with a roommate. I want to live with an intimate partner. Nothing will dive bomb intimacy like a lack of trust. If you can't trust your spouse, it will be very difficult to find intimacy with them. In the right circumstances, a lack of trust may be warranted. Cheating, porn addiction and similar cases fall into those circumstances. In many cases however, it is jealousy or insecurity that fuel a lack of trust. Let's do some self-evaluation. Do you always have to know everything your spouse did throughout the day? Do you trust them to have their own social media account? Do you fight over them talking with someone of the opposite sex? Do you go through their phone to see who they have texted or talked to? These are all toxic behaviors that scream, I don't trust you. Why are they toxic? Because, lack of trust kills intimacy. What do we do when we are insecure in a relationship? We beef up the security. We behave and act in ways to protect ourselves.

The sad part is, this not only kills intimacy; it kills marriages. In an effort to feel more secure, you push your spouse further away. Do you come home to a warden that bosses you around or do you come home to a lover and a friend? Trust is very important in our relationship with God. The bible makes it extremely clear that we should trust the Lord. Proverbs 3:5 and 6 reads, "Trust in the Lord with all thine heart; and lean not unto thine own understanding. In all thy ways acknowledge Him, and He shall direct thy paths." God desires relationship with us. He loves us like a father, a brother and a friend. For us to be this close with God, we must trust Him. It all falls apart without trust. Think about the trust of a child. My children are very loving and intimate with Brandy and me. They can fall asleep in our arms in complete peace because they inexplicably trust us. We need to display this same kind of trust and confidence in God. Sometimes insecurity with a spouse can reflect an insecurity toward God. Sometimes our lack of trust points to a larger issue of where we are at spiritually. Transparency is a great thing in marriage. We should know a great deal about each other. Transparency is not good however when it is demanded. When it leads to a total lack of privacy. When it leads to toxic behaviors.

These behaviors don't work. They will never give you a better marriage. Work hard and love deeply. Promote trust within your marriage. Promote an atmosphere of intimacy. Isn't that what you really want?

The Challenge

Identify and address any cases where trust is an issue. Rate your intimacy level with each other on a ten scale. 0 being no intimacy and 10 being completely intimate. Discuss how you can get your marriage higher on the scale. Pray and ask God to promote trust and intimacy in your marriage. Pray that you become more intimate with Him.

41. I Need A Vacation

I need a vacation. Have you ever said that before? I believe everyone who lives in reality has. Vacation is such a blessing. It is healthy in so many ways. No, you do not need a vacation from your marriage. That is not where this one is going. Your marriage needs a vacation from everything else. I have always seen vacation as a reward. I work hard to make money and spend a lot of time doing it. My reward is to take some time and money and have some fun with it. Think about this concept within your marriage. You work hard at it. You sacrifice and do, so it will turn out great. Maybe it's time to take your marriage and have some fun with it. Reward yourselves for a job well done. I grew up in a family who cherished their vacations. My parents worked hard, and they looked forward to those times to get away. My dad would say, "We are getting out of the city limits." He wanted to get out of the everyday norm. That doesn't mean the norm wasn't good. The everyday norm of your marriage should be good, fun, and rewarding. But sometimes we need to get out of the city limits. Sometimes we need to create a new experience. An experience is a great investment. They give us something to look forward to and something precious to look back on. Creating new memories will last a lifetime. This is a blessing from God. In Ecclesiastes, Solomon mostly talks about how life has frustrated and disappointed him. He does however find contentment. In Ecclesiastes 2:24 it says, "There is nothing better for a man, than that he should eat and drink, and that he should make his soul enjoy good in his labor. This also I saw that it was from the hand of God." What was from the hand of God? That a man should enjoy the good of his labor. If you have not worked hard for your marriage, then you are not deserving of enjoyment. You have robbed yourself of this blessing. If you have worked hard for your marriage than you should enjoy what it has produced. You should take your spouse by the hand, stick your feet in the sand in congratulate each other on your success. Think about the retired life. Being able to relax of a front porch rocking chair feeling good about working hard all your life. Putting your feet up and enjoying life. This is your reward. We never retire from marriage. We should however find its reward. Let it take its vacations. Let it put its feet up every once in a while. Create a new experience. Create a lasting memory. Have some fun.

The Challenge

Plan some vacations for your marriage. Plan some simple ones. Plan some big ones. Reward yourselves for making it this far. Pray that God will help you enjoy the good of your labor. Thank God for the new experiences that are coming down the road.

42. Taco Tuesday

Everybody loves taco Tuesday. Ok, maybe not everybody. If your one of those people that doesn't like Mexican food that's ok. This devotion isn't about tacos. It's about what taco Tuesday can do for your marriage. I'm talking about the intentional act of sitting down at the table together as a family on a regular basis. No phones, no television, no distractions. This is a powerful tool for your marriage. When we schedule a gathering around food, it is usually a positive engagement. Who doesn't like eating? It's a great way to unwind and enjoy some good fellowship with people you care about. It works the same for elderly couples and young couples. It works the same all over the world; no matter your race or background. With the rich and with the poor. For the better and for the worst. In sickness or in health. No matter what life gives us, we can all find fulfillment at the table. In Psalm 23:5 David told the Lord; "You prepare a table before me in the presents of my enemies; you anoint my head with oil; my cup runs over." David said that God prepared him a table. When David needed Him most, God prepared a table. In the presents of our enemies, much like David, we become wore out. We become stressed, burdened, and tired. God knew what David needed. He needed Taco Tuesday. He needed a set apart time to sit down with his God to eat and fellowship. He needed to recharge. No distractions. Oh, that we would experience this kind of intimacy with God. God desires to fellowship with you. In your good times and in your darkest moments. Taco Tuesday doesn't fix everything. Your problems will still be there when you get up from the table. It does however help you recharge and remember what you are fighting for. Even if your marriage is going through hard times and you can't seem to agree on anything. Be extremely intentional about keeping the kitchen table a positive place. A place you can let your guard down and relax. This is something we all need to thrive. Before the first bite is taken, stop and take time to thank God for what He has prepared for you. What a blessed place your table will be if everyone who sat at it understood where their blessings came from. God has prepared a table for you and for your marriage. Won't you sit down and partake of it?

The Challenge

If you don't regularly sit down as a family to eat, make in a new venture. If you already do, try to think of ways you can make it a more positive experience for your marriage. Before you take the first bite, thank God for what you have been given.

43. Revelation

We receive revelation when something comes into our hearts and minds that wasn't there before. A trigger goes off and the way we start to look at something changes. If you are a Christian, then you know this happened when you began to put your faith in Christ. You received revelation about who Jesus was. You changed. I want to illustrate this using Isaiah 53:2. It says, "For He shall grow up before him as a tender plant, and as a root out of dry ground: He hath no form nor comeliness; and when we shall see Him, there is no beauty that we should desire Him." That scripture is talking about Jesus. How can it be? No comeliness? No Beauty? That's not true. It is not true to you and me because we have received revelation. Jesus is beautiful to me because I know who He is and what He has done. It wasn't always that way with me. It wasn't always that way with you. There is a whole world out there that does not see the beauty that we see in Christ. This kind of revelation exist around the idea of marriage as well. There is a world out there that does not see marriage as beautiful as God sees it. Marriage is quite ugly in some people's eyes. Are they right, or have they not received the correct revelation? Adam received a revelation the first time he laid his eyes on Eve. It is also important to note that he said this before the sin and fall. He got a revelation that I believe was true and given to him by his creator. In Genesis 2:23 Adam said, "This is now bone of my bones, and flesh of my flesh: she shall be called Woman, because she was taken out of man." This revelation was pure. He was not trying to impress her. He simply said what was laid on his heart. She was not just a companion. She was not just a helper. She was not just a sexual partner. She was part of who he was. Bone of his bones. He could not be his whole self without her. This revelation can do more for your marriage then about any other if you could only receive it. Is your marriage just something you have? Is your spouse just someone you put up with? Or are they part of what makes you who you are? Adams response to seeing his wife shows responsibility, commitment and devotion. That's my wife, and she is beautiful. Just as you discovered the beauty of Christ, I want you to see how beautiful your marriage is to God despite what the world around you says. Are you ready for revelation?

The Challenge

This challenge revolves around prayer. The correct way to see marriage as God does must be revealed by Him. Pray consistently that God will bring you revelation. Ask Him to allow you to see your marriage as He does. Prepare yourself to receive what God has to show you.

44. Wise Counsel

Have you ever gotten any bad advice? Did you act on that advice and find out exactly how bad it was? I have gotten some pretty rotten marriage advice over the years. It seems that everyone that has been married has an opinion on how you should do it. I had a close friend tell me once, "you go home and tell her that this is the way it's going to be." That advice didn't work out so well for me. Some of the worst marital advice you can get can come from those closest to you. I'm not saying that they don't care about you or that they are not trying to help. Caring about you is not enough. They need to care about your marriage. Take marriage advice from people that put your marriage first and you second. Let that one sink in. Don't be afraid to get marriage advice. Just get it from someone that has a passion for their own marriage and a strong will to do it right. Proverbs 20:18 reads, "Every purpose is established by counsel: and with good advice make war." When you're having marriage problems or you have to make a big decision, establish that decision with wise counsel. Don't make war on horrible advice. You will lose. Think of a war movie and all the generals standing in the war room looking over maps of the battlefield. They all have an angle that they see it from. That is why they are all important to gain the victory. Bringing in wise counsel into your situation can bring a new angle and shed some much needed light. Of course, you can always go to your heavenly Father in prayer. He is a good counselor. Let's look at another verse in Proverbs. Proverbs 11:14 says, "Where no counsel is, the people fall: but in the multitude of counselors there is safety." A fall or safety. Which one do you want for your marriage? The people who refuse counsel will fall. The odds are stacked against them.

This is true for all of life, not just marriage. But safety exist in the multitude of counselors. Every marriage needs a support system around it. That's what the church is all about. It exists so that believers can help one another navigate through life. God established this because He knows we will need each other to succeed at being His people and at having blessed marriages and families. The church can be an incredible resource for your marriage if you will choose to use it. Surround your marriage with wise people that you can call on when you're in need. People that will not look down on you but will care enough about your marriage to help it succeed. Don't be embarrassed about seeking counsel. Any good counsel you get will be from someone that understands the struggle. Counsel should not just be a last resort when you're having problems. It should be an active part of any marriage. Seek safety. Seek counsel. Gain victory.

The Challenge

Think it over and come up with a few people or couples that you believe are wise and that care about your marriage. If you can't think of any then go to church and find them. They are out there. Pray that God will surround your marriage with wise counsel and that you will recognize when you need it.

The End

The end of this book; not your marriage.
Stay married. Stay blessed.

Made in the USA
Columbia, SC
15 January 2025